KNOW-IT-ALLS

DINOSAURS!

Written by Jay Johnson

Illustrated by Greg Harris

AN AMERICAN GREETINGS COMPANY

Manufactured for Learning Horizons, Inc.
One American Road, Cleveland, OH 44144. Printed in China.
Fabriqué pour Learning Horizons, Inc.
One American Road, Cleveland, OH 44144.
Fabriqué en Chine.
Cover & interior design © 2001 Learning Horizons, Inc.

Visit us at: www.learninghorizons.com

MILLIONS OF YEARS AGO

You see a lot of dinosaurs in movies and on TV shows. But do you think those are real dinosaurs?

DINO TIMELINE

First Dinosaurs Appear
225 MYA

208 MYA

MYA = Millon Years Ago | **Triassic Period**

| **Jurassic Period**

Real dinosaurs are *extinct*—that means they are dead and gone forever. Dinosaurs were animals, in the same big group as birds and crocodiles. They lived on earth a very long time ago—way before people.

144 MYA			Dinosaurs Become Extinct 65 MYA	First People Appear 40,000 YEARS AGO
Cretaceous Period				Today

ROCKY RECORDS

How do we know dinosaurs really lived on earth? Scientists called **paleontologists** study **fossils**. Fossils are the remains of things that lived millions of years ago. These remains have become part of rocks buried in the earth.

There are many fossils of dinosaur tracks, bones, skin, and even eggs! In fact, scientists find a new dino fossil about every six weeks!

Over 700 kinds of dinosaurs have been identified. Most of them have been found in the past 25 years.

DINOSAUR MEALS

POLACANTHUS (PLANT-EATER)

Most kinds of dinosaurs ate only *plants*. Many of them had gigantic bodies with huge stomachs. And some had long necks to reach leafy treetops.

Other kinds of dinos ate only *meat*—lizards, insects, and other dinosaurs. Most meat-eaters ran on two feet, rather than four. They were fast runners, which helped them catch their dinner. Some meat-eaters were big, but some were as small as chickens!

BARYONYX (MEAT-EATER)

A few kinds of dinosaurs ate both meat and plants. They liked variety!

ALLOSAURUS

(AL-o-SAW-rus)

Allosaurus was fierce. It was one of the biggest, strongest meat-eaters of its time. It had large teeth with edges like saw blades. Its head was as big as a first-grader!

This dinosaur weighed up to 2 tons (1.8 metric tons). It was about 35 feet (11 m) long and 9 feet (3 m) tall at the hips.

Some people believe that *Allosaurus* looked for food—usually other dinosaurs—in a group of hunters called a **pack.**

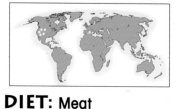

WHEN IT LIVED: About 150 million years ago, Jurassic Period

FOSSILS FOUND IN: Colorado, Wyoming, Utah, Oklahoma, New Mexico

DIET: Meat

BRACHIOSAURUS

(BRACK-ee-o-SAW-rus)

Like the giraffe, this dinosaur had long front legs and a superlong neck so it could nibble leaves from the highest tree branches. Its head rose up to 60 feet (18 m) off the ground—that's as high as a four-story building!

This four-legged dinosaur was a giant, weighing up to 80 tons (72.5 metric tons). *Brachiosaurus* grew an amazing 100 feet (30.5 m) long. The length of three of these dinosaurs would equal one football field!

Brachiosaurus may have had a good sense of smell because it had huge nostrils—on top of its head!

STEGOSAURUS

(STEG-o-SAW-rus)

Stegosaurus had a tail as long as its elephant-sized body (about 30 feet or 9 meters). With four sharp spines, the tail could be used as a great club to fight off meat-eaters!

Stegosaurus also had a double row of triangular plates from its neck to its tail. The plates probably helped protect the dinosaur from being eaten! Some of the plates were as small as saucers. Others were as big as truck wheels!

WHEN IT LIVED:
About 150 million years ago, Jurassic Period

FOSSILS FOUND IN:
Western North America

DIET: Plants

ALLOSAURUS

IGUANODON
(ig-WAN-o-don)

Chomp, chomp, chomp! *Iguanodon* was the first plant-eating dino whose fossils were discovered in modern times. They were found in England in 1825.

Iguanodons traveled together in herds that grazed along the edges of swamps and lakes. Their strong grinding teeth chewed up juicy ferns and reeds.

This dinosaur was heavy. It weighed up to 6 tons (5.5 metric tons). It was 33 feet (10 m) long and taller than two grownups balancing on each other's shoulders!

VELOCIRAPTOR

(ve-LOSS-uh-RAP-ter)

Velociraptor lived in deserts. It had large eyes. It may have needed big eyes to hunt at night. It probably ate lizards and other small animals, tiny baby dinosaurs (called **hatchlings**), and eggs.

PROTOCERATOPS

Velociraptor means "swift robber." This dino was smart and fast! It had a large slashing toe and hand claws. Its second-toe claw was 4 inches (10 cm) long. *Velociraptor's* body grew to about 6 feet (2 m) long, the size of a large dog. Very bad doggie!

WHEN IT LIVED:
About 75–80 million years ago, Cretaceous Period

FOSSILS FOUND IN:
Mongolia and China

DIET: You know...meat!

TRICERATOPS

(try-SAIR-a-tops)

Knights in the Middle Ages used armor to protect themselves in battle. *Triceratops* also had an armor-covered face for protection—and three sharp horns! Its name means "three-horned head."

Triceratops also had a big frill of bone. This frill may have protected the neck and shoulders from attacks. Or it may have just been for show, like a peacock's feathers.

WHEN IT LIVED: About 65–70 million years ago, Cretaceous Period

FOSSILS FOUND IN: Western North America

DIET: Plants

TYRANNOSAURUS

This dino chewed on ferns, palms, and other plants. And it ate a lot of them! *Triceratops* weighed almost 6 tons (5.5 metric tons) and was about 30 feet (9 m) long. That's as big as an elephant!

WHEN IT LIVED:

About 67–100 million years ago, Cretaceous Period

FOSSILS FOUND IN:

North America and Asia

DIET: Meat

TYRANNOSAURUS

(tie-RAN-o-SAW-rus)

Tyrannosaurus was the fiercest meat-eating dinosaur. It wasn't the biggest, but it was huge—7 tons (6.5 metric tons) of charging monster. At over 40 feet (12 m) long, it was a smart killer with sharp eyesight.

This dinosaur's head was over 5 feet (1.5 m) long. Its muscular mouth was filled with 50 sharp, jagged teeth. The biggest teeth were the size of bananas! Its front limbs were strong, but they were so short they couldn't even reach up to its mouth.

SINOSAUROPTERYX

(SIN-o-sar-OP-terix)

Sinosauropteryx was a birdlike dinosaur with big eyes like an owl and a narrow head like a pheasant. It was a little over 3 feet (1 m) long and about as tall as a grownup's knee. *Sinosauropteryx* was a swift little creature that probably ate insects and lizards as well as plants that grew close to the ground.

WHEN IT LIVED:
About 135 million years ago, Cretaceous Period

FOSSILS FOUND IN:
China

DIET: Meat and plants

Did you know that today's birds are called "living dinosaurs"? That's because they developed from small dinosaurs, like *Sinosauropteryx*, millions of years ago!

Why did all the dinos disappear? Did the great meteor that hit the earth kill them? Or did they vanish because of disease?

No one knows for certain!